Made In Uganda

In Support of Uganda's Children

Printed and bound by New Vision
Kampala, Uganda

Tendo's Wish

Written by: Cathy Kreutter

Art Work by:

Johnmary Mukiza & Eric Kreutter

Published by:
CORNERSTONE DEVELOPMENT
P.O. Box 9242, Kampala, Uganda
E-mail: info@oldmzeebook.com

In association with:
NORTH STAR PUBLISHERS LTD.
Plot 13, Acol Enoka Road, Lira Municipality, Uganda
P.O Box 376, Kampala, Uganda
E-mail: northstarpublishers@gmail.com

Order online: Amazon.com

Special thanks to: Sharlee Curry, and Els de Temmerman for editing and consultation.

Back Page: All photos taken by Dani Lynn Walker Kreutter
(except children with firewood, by Sharlee Curry)

Copyright: Cathy Kreutter 2016
First printing: 2015. New Vision Printing: Kampala, Uganda
ISBN (HB): 9-780692-500569

www.OldMzeeBook.com

Dedicated to:

Leo

By the time the rooster crowed, Tendo was already awake and had:

Released the chickens

Washed the dishes

Fetched water

Swept the compound

Wrapped his breakfast

Bathed and dressed

Organized his books

Tied firewood

But just one more thing...

"I wish I had a pair of black school shoes.

And a tin of polish would be nice!"

Tendo grabbed the firewood bundle
for the school cooks,
threw on a few extra sticks,
and ran off to school.

"Good Morning!"

he cheerily greeted other people
on the road as he dashed past.

Tendo then took a
short cut to school
so he could...

...stop by Jajja's house.

"Hello Jajja I brought you some firewood!"

"Eh, webale Tendo,
you are such a kind boy,
I needed some firewood to finish my cooking."

"Glad I could help. Bye!"

So Jajja finished frying her chapatis
and started down the road to the market,
when she met...

...a knife sharpener who was standing with his pockets all turned out.

"Hello, what is the matter?"

"I was looking for breakfast money and found a hole in my pocket instead!"

So Jajja gave him one of her fresh chapatis.

"Eh, webale, how can I pay you?"

"Don't worry, glad I could help."

The knife sharpener peddled down the road to town and came upon...

...a farmer in her banana patch sitting on an old tree stump.

"Hello, what is the matter?"

"My panga is dull and I can't harvest this ripe bunch of bananas"

So the knife sharpener carefully sharpened the blade for the farmer.

"Eh webale, how can I pay you?"

"Don't worry, glad I could help."

The farmer harvested her bananas and walked towards the market when she met...

...a worried carpenter with a wailing child attached to his leg.

"Hello, what is the matter?"

"I finished repairing my sister's window and her child does not want me to go!"

"Give him two bananas to distract him"

"Eh webale, how can I pay you?"

"Don't worry, glad I could help."

The carpenter then walked to his favorite restaurant for lunch and came upon...

...a tailor trying to prop up her shade with a broom.

"Hello, what is the matter?"

"My wobbly pole finally fell and I have so much sewing today!"

"I can fix that easily."

"Eh, webale, how can I pay you?"

"Don't worry, glad I could help."

So the tailor went back to her sewing when she saw...

...a very embarrassed

boda-boda driver.

"Hello, what is the matter?"

"My trousers split and
I can't ride with my underwear showing"

"Bring your trousers here, I can help!"

So the tailor expertly sewed his trouser seams back together.

"Eh, webale, how can I pay you?"

"Don't worry, glad I could help."

The boda-boda then rode off
when he saw...

...a nurse running down the road.

"Hello, what is the matter?"

"I am going to be late for my afternoon shift at the hospital!"

"Hop on, I can get you there faster!"

"Eh, webale, how can I pay you?"

"Don't worry, glad I could help"

The nurse sat comfortably on the passenger seat and when they reached her stop she heard...

...the shoe cobbler yelling and holding up a throbbing thumb!

"Hello Mzee, what is the matter?"

"These pesky flies! It was a slow day so I repaired these old school shoes my son outgrew years ago. A fly distracted me and I hit myself!"

So the nurse bandaged up his thumb.

"Eh, webale, how can I pay you?"

"Don't worry, glad I could help"

The mzee decided to pack up his tools for the day when he saw...

...three school children walking home talking and laughing.

The one in the middle reminded him of his son.

"Hmmmmmmmm"

thought the shoe cobbler...

"WEBALE NYO, MZEE!"

And Tendo ran home amazed at the kindness of the old shoe cobbler.

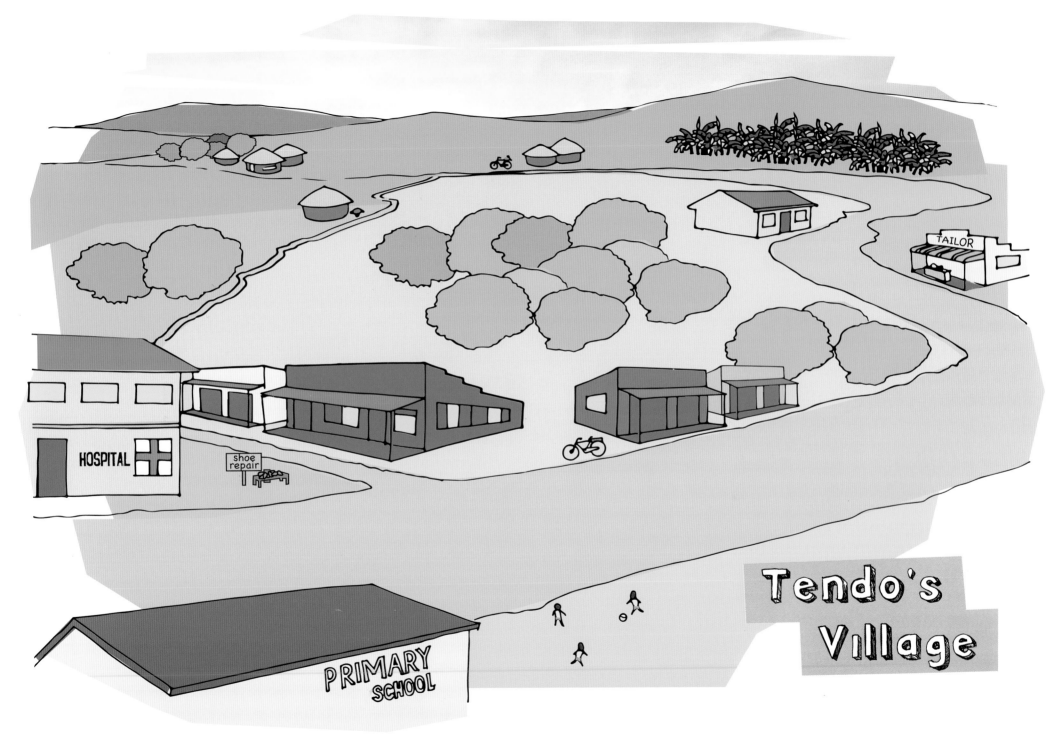

HOSPITAL

shoe repair

TAILOR

PRIMARY SCHOOL

Tendo's Village

A kindness that
is given is eventually
returned.

Cobbler

Knife sharpener

Children off to school

Banana vendor

Tailor

Carpenter

Boda boda

Farmer

Chapati vendor

Nurse

Glossary

Mzee: *Mmm-zay,*
A term of respect for older men in Swahili - an East African language.

Jajja: *Jah - jah*
Means 'grandparent' in local Luganda dialect.

Chapatis: *Chah-paht-tees*
A delicious flat bread that is fried and eaten any time of day.

Webale: *Weh-bah-leh*
"Thank you."

Eh, Webale: *Eh, weh-bah-le*
A surprised "thank you."

Webale Nyo: *Weh-bah-leh nyo*
"Thank you very much."

Panga: *Pang-ga,*
A machete used for farming.

Boda-boda: *Bo-dah, Bo-dah*
A bicycle/motorcycle taxi that is a popular mode of transport!

An Extra Challenge...

1. On the village map, identify **Tendo's** house and the shortcut he takes to school. Can you follow the direction of the kindness journey and where all the other characters meet each other.

2. Now that you have read the story, go back and look at the pages of **Tendo** running at the beginning and the end. Can you identify all the characters in the book that **Tendo** passes?

3. Can you find the hidden reference to the book, **"I Know an Old Mzee Who Swallowed A Fly?"**

Of interest to the reader:

This is a story about kindness and community. Each character gave a small kindness that was passed on while not knowing that they were playing a part in Tendo's morning wish. Imagine what a nice world we'd have if we each did small acts of kindness every day!

Ugandans are generous people. According to the World Giving Index 2014, with data collected by Gallup, on the African continent, Uganda ranks the third most generous!

Many schools in Uganda have been using firewood for cooking meals. However, the Ministry of Education, and many conservation organizations are now promoting energy efficient stoves, or the use of biogas to protect the environment.

Boda-Bodas started back in the 1980's ferrying people on bicycles between the immigration offices on the Kenya Uganda border. The name comes from moving "border to border". Motorcycles have now taken over bicycles as boda-bodas and are all over Uganda.

The knife sharpener is a mobile knife sharpening business where one sits backwards on a bicycle seat and pedals to turn the disk while holding the knife carefully at an angle to sharpen.

South Sudan

D.R. Congo

UGANDA

Kenya

Tanzania

Rwanda & Burundi

All proceeds of this book go towards school fees for students in Uganda. For more information about Uganda, the authors or the school fees program visit:

www.oldmzeebook.com.